Helen Keller

By Pamela Walker

Children's Press
A Division of Scholastic Inc.
New York / Toronto / London / Auckland / Sydney
Mexico City / New Delhi / Hong Kong
Danbury, Connecticut

Photo Credits: Cover, pp. 5 (photo), 9, 11, 15, American Foundation for the Blind; pp. 5 (frame), 17 (frame) © Image Farm; pp. 7, 13, 17 (photo), 19, 21 © Corbis
Contributing Editor: Jennifer Silate
Book Design: Victoria Johnson

Visit Children's Press on the Internet at:
http://publishing.grolier.com

Library of Congress Cataloging-in-Publication Data

Walker, Pamela, 1958-
 Helen Keller / by Pamela Walker.
    p. cm. -- (Real people)
   ISBN 0-516-23434-X (lib. bdg.) -- ISBN 0-516-23588-5 (pbk.)
   1. Keller, Helen, 1880-1968--Juvenile literature. 2. Blind-deaf women--United States--Biography--Juvenile literature. 3. Blind-deaf--United States--Biography--Juvenile literature. 4. Sullivan, Annie, 1866-1936--Juvenile literature. [1. Keller, Helen, 1880-1968. 2. Blind. 3. Deaf. 4. Physically handicapped. 5. Women--Biography.] I. Title.

 HV1624.K4 W35 2001
 362.4'1'092--dc21

                                        2001017268

Contents

Meet Helen Keller.

5

Helen was **blind**.

She could not see.

Helen was **deaf**.

She could not hear.

Helen had a good **teacher**.

Her name was Annie Sullivan.

Annie helped Helen learn new things.

Annie helped Helen learn to spell.

Helen used her fingers to spell words.

Helen also learned to use her fingers to read words.

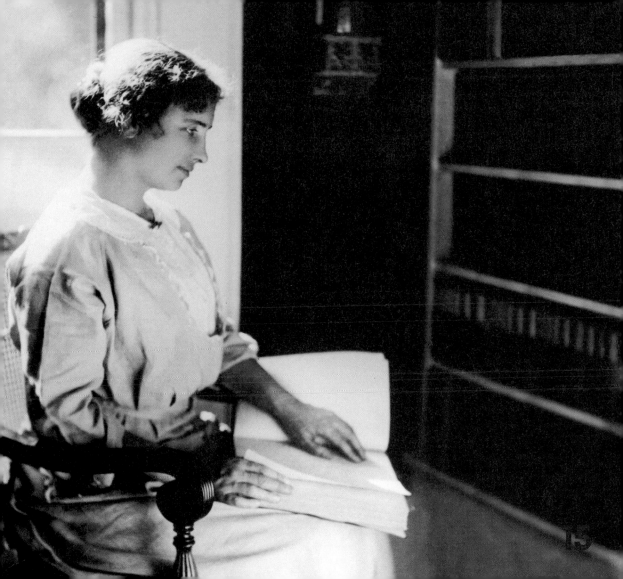

Helen learned a lot.

She even **graduated** from **college**.

17

Helen talked to many people.

She told them what it is like to be deaf and blind.

Helen Keller helped many people.

New Words

blind (**blynd**) unable to see

college (**kahl**-ihj) a school where you can study after high school

deaf (**dehf**) unable to hear

graduated (**graj**-oo-ayt-uhd) having finished the course of studies of a college or school

teacher (**tee**-chuhr) a person who teaches

To Find Out More

Books
Helen Keller: Crusader for the Blind and Deaf
by Stewart Graff
Dell Publishing

Helen Keller: Courage in the Dark
by Johanna Hurwitz
Demco Media, Limited

Web Site
Helen Keller
http://www.csnmail.net/~missE/helenkeller.htm
At this Web site you can read about Helen Keller's life.
You can also find answers to kids' questions about what
it is like to be blind.

Index

About the Author

Pamela Walker was born in Kentucky. When she grew up, she moved to New York and became a writer.

Reading Consultants

Kris Flynn, Coordinator, Small School District Literacy, The San Diego County Office of Education

Shelly Forys, Certified Reading Recovery Specialist, W.J. Zahnow Elementary School, Waterloo, IL

Sue McAdams, Certified Reading Recovery Specialist and Literary Consultant, Dallas, TX